Holiday Jokes

KU-328-824

Sandy Ransford

Illustrated by *Gerald Hawksley*

MACMILLAN CHILDREN'S BOOKS

First published 2002
by Macmillan Children's Books
a division of Macmillan Publishers Ltd
20 New Wharf Road, London N1 9RR
Basingstoke and Oxford
www.panmacmillan.com

Associated companies throughout the world

ISBN 0 330 39771 0

1 3 5 7 9 8 6 4 2

A CIP catalogue record for this book is available from the British Library.

Printed by Mackays of Chatham plc, Chatham, Kent.

Contents

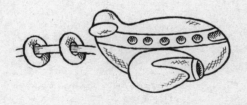

En Route

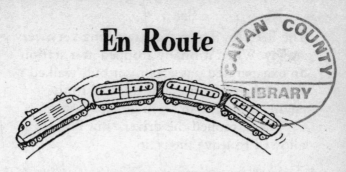

SIGN ON A TRAVEL AGENT'S: Please go away.

TICKET COLLECTOR: I'm sorry, sir, this
ticket is for Blackpool and the train is going
to Cleethorpes.

PASSENGER: I want to go to Bournemouth.
Shall I take this train?
**GUARD: You can if you like, but the driver
will be along in a minute.**

TICKET COLLECTOR: I'm sorry, sir, this
ticket is for Blackpool and the train is going
to Cleethorpes.
**PASSENGER: Oh dear. Does the driver
know he's going the wrong way?**

PASSENGER: I want to catch a late train to
Edinburgh.
**BOOKING CLERK: Take the 9.15. That's
usually as late as any.**

PASSENGER: Is this train on time?
GUARD: We're happy if it's on the track, sir.

1

The 8.15 for Truro was travelling very, very slowly. When it finally stopped at a station an exasperated passenger got out, walked down the platform, and shouted to the engine driver, 'Can't you go any faster?'

'I can,' replied the driver. 'But I'm not allowed to leave the train.'

How can you tell when the train has gone? It leaves tracks behind.

MRS DIM: Was your train crowded?
MRS DUMB: At first, yes. Our carriage was very full. But when it stopped at a station we spotted that the next carriage was empty so we all got out and moved into that.

When a train stopped at a station in the centre of a small town, the platform guard rushed to the nearby greengrocer's. 'Help!' he shouted. 'I've lost the pea out of my whistle! Can you give me another one, please?'

But the greengrocer only had split peas, so the guard put one of those in his whistle and dashed back to the station. When he blew the whistle, only half the train moved out of the station.

Why did the train go 'ouch!'?
It had a tender behind.

MRS SAUSAGETUM: I'm afraid my son has
swallowed our tickets.
**TICKET COLLECTOR: Then I suggest you
buy him a second helping.**

PASSENGER: I'd like a return ticket, please.
BOOKING CLERK: Where to?
PASSENGER: Back here, of course.

A little old lady was travelling to stay with
her daughter by the seaside. Opposite her sat
a young man, chewing gum and staring into
space. The old lady looked at him for a
while, and then said, 'I'm afraid it's no use
talking to me, young man, I'm stone-deaf.'

PORTER: I had a tremendous struggle getting
that woman's luggage on the Brighton train.
HIS COLLEAGUE: Why, was it very heavy?
PORTER: No, but she wanted to go to
Margate.

SIGN AT A RAILWAY STATION:
Will passengers please not cross the lines.
Underneath someone had scrawled: **Because
it takes ages to uncross them.**

NERVOUS PASSENGER: Which end of the
train should I get off?
TICKET COLLECTOR: **Either, it stops at
both ends.**

A man encumbered by a lot of luggage was
rushing along the platform but, even as he
approached it, the train slowly but surely
made its way out of the station. A passing
porter sympathized. 'Did you just miss your
train, sir?'

'No!' exclaimed the man. 'I didn't like the
look of it so I chased it out of the station.'

A guard was explaining to some waiting
passengers, 'This train goes to Inverness and
points north.'

An exasperated passenger replied, 'I want
a train to Stirling and I don't care which way
it points.'

ANNIE: Did you enjoy going to Little Birdingham?
DANNY: Yes, but the town was so small that when the train stopped at the station its engine was out in the country.

A large man got off a train and said to a porter, 'Please call me a taxi.'

The porter replied, 'OK, you're a taxi, but you look more like a ten tonne truck to me.'

Some twins were getting rather bored with their father's slow driving round the twisty Cornish lanes. Eventually young Ben piped up, 'Dad, let Len drive. It's much more exciting when he does.'

The Millington-Mills were staying in a holiday apartment in the south of France, and had hired a car in which to tour around and see the sights. One evening, young Mervyn Millington-Mills had a date, and asked his father if he could borrow the car.

'Whatever for?' asked his father. 'It's only five minutes' walk into town! What do you think your feet are for?'

'One for the accelerator and one for the brake,' replied young Mervyn.

'He took the bus home from his holidays, but his mum made him take it back.'

The Roundtums had rushed off to the airport and arrived just as their flight was being called. 'I wish we'd brought the piano with us,' said Mrs Roundtum.

'Whatever for?' asked Mr Roundtum.

'I left the tickets on it.'

NERVOUS PASSENGER: I've never flown before. You will get us down safely, won't you?

PILOT: I've not left anyone up there yet.

When would you be glad to be down and out?

After a bumpy flight in a plane.

JANE: I hate being up there in a plane.

WAYNE: I'd hate to be up there without one.

How do ghosts travel?

By British Scareways.

What's yellow and white and travels at 500 mph?
A pilot's egg sandwich.

What's big and hairy and flies very fast?
King Kongcorde.

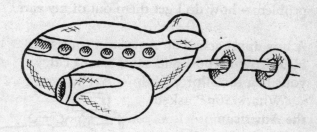

An old lady was on her first flight and feeling rather nervous. 'What happens if we run out of fuel?' she asked a stewardess.

Another passenger butted in. 'We all get out and push,' he grinned.

TERRY: Can you telephone from a plane?
JERRY: Of course I can tell a phone from a plane!

What do you get if you cross an apple with a plane?
Pie in the sky.

One passenger on the plane complained about her ears popping. 'Have these boiled sweets,' said the stewardess.

After the flight the stewardess asked her how she was feeling.

'I feel fine,' she replied. 'The sweets stopped the popping, but there's just one problem – how do I get them out of my ears?'

A boy approached an American tourist at Heathrow Airport and said, 'Can I carry your bag for 50p?'

'What's 50p?' asked the American.

'You're right,' replied the boy. 'Make it a fiver.'

'I just flew in from Florida.'
'Aren't your arms tired?'

VINNIE: I don't travel by plane.
MINNIE: Why not?
VINNIE: The journey to the airport makes me car sick.

TRAVELLER: How much to take me to the airport?
TAXI DRIVER: £20.
TRAVELLER: And how much to take my suitcase?
TAXI DRIVER: **Nothing for your suitcase.**
TRAVELLER: OK, you take the suitcase and I'll walk.

PILOT: Mayday, mayday, my port engine is on fire.
AIR TRAFFIC CONTROL: **State your height and position.**
PILOT: I'm five foot nine and sitting in the cockpit.

MRS GUBBINS: Oh dear, this is a very bumpy flight.
MRS BUGGINS: **We haven't left the runway yet.**

Definition of the jet age: **Breakfast in Paris, lunch in New York, dinner in Los Angeles, luggage in Moscow.**

Definition of air travel: **A way of seeing less and less of more and more.**

PILOT: Ladies and gentlemen, we have just flown from Heathrow to Rome in one hour and twenty-five minutes.
PASSENGER: **That must be a record!**
PILOT: No, this is your captain speaking to you live from the flight deck.

How did the frog cross the Channel?
By hoppercraft.

'How many meals did you have on the cross-Channel ferry?'
'Four.'
'Four? That sounds a lot for such a short journey.'
'Yes, well it was two down and two up.'

What stops at the bottom of the ocean with fifty people on board?
An octobus.

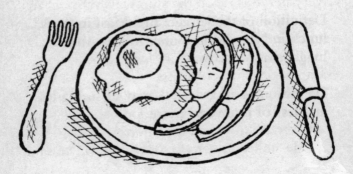

A man was hanging on to the rail of a ship as it tossed over the waves. A passing steward asked if he was all right.

'No,' replied the man. 'I feel terrible. What shall I do?'

'You'll soon find out,' replied the steward.

What's the difference between seasickness and an auction?

One is the effects of a sail, the other a sale of effects.

Which part of a ship is like Anne Robinson?
The stern.

How does a ship listen?
Through its engineers.

An old lady went on her first cruise. She felt very nervous when the ship was right out in the middle of the ocean and they could see nothing but sea.

'How far are we from land?' she asked one of the ship's officers.

'About three miles,' he replied.

She felt relieved. 'Oh, good,' she answered. 'In which direction?'

He smiled at her. 'Er, downwards,' he said.

There was a young lady from China
Who travelled the seas on a liner.
She slipped on the deck,
And twisted her neck,
And now she can see what's behind her.

What do you call someone who crosses the
Atlantic from east to west and then from
west to east without taking a bath or a
shower?
A dirty double-crosser.

'I was once
shipwrecked and lived
on a tin of sardines for
a week.'
**'I'm surprised you
didn't fall off.'**

MRS MINIVER: If this
boat were to sink, who
would you save first, me or the children?
MR MINIVER: Me.

Knock, knock.
Who's there?
Dwayne.
Dwayne who?
Dwayne the ocean, I'm dwowning.

NERVOUS PASSENGER: Do these ships sink often?
CAPTAIN: No, only once.

CRUISE PASSENGER: They've dropped the anchor.
HER FRIEND: I thought they might. It's been dangling there all day.

LILY: I hear the ferry men are striking for shorter hours.
MILLY: They're right. I always thought sixty minutes was too long for an hour.

TERRY: On what date did you cross the Atlantic?
JERRY: I didn't cross on a date, I crossed on a boat.

Seeing the Sights

ANNE: When you were in London did you see them changing the Guard?
JAN: No, were they dirty?

A man went on a motoring holiday with a friend, who got perturbed when the driver shut his eyes every time they approached a red light. 'Why do you do that?' he asked.

'Oh,' he replied, 'when you've seen one red light you've seen them all.'

SIGN AT APPROACH TO BATH:
Bath welcomes careful drivers. One man in Britain is knocked down every thirty minutes. Underneath someone had scrawled: And he's getting awfully fed up with it.

'Don't complain about the traffic. If there were fewer cars on the roads it would be even harder to find a parking place.'

How do you get two whales in a mini?
Over the Severn Bridge (to Wales).

A man knocked on the door of a bed-and-breakfast establishment. 'Can you give me a room for the night and a bath, please?' he asked.

'I can give you a room but you'll have to take your own bath,' replied the landlady.

Jimmy went on a camping trip. 'Did your tent leak?' asked his friend Timmy.

'Only when it rained,' replied Jimmy.

A tourist stopped a local man and asked, 'Am I on the right road for Shakespeare's birthplace?'

'Yes,' replied the man. 'But there's no need to hurry, he's dead.'

An American visiting a Cotswold village struck up a conversation with one of its residents. 'And how old is your oldest inhabitant?' he asked.

'We don't have one,' replied the native. 'He died last week.'

FIRST MAN: I'm a stranger round here. Where's the nearest boozer?
SECOND MAN: You're talking to him.

MRS DIBBLE: We're going to Bury St Edmunds at Easter.
MRS DOBBLE: I didn't even know he was dead.

Why is the Isle of Wight a fraud?
It has Cowes you can't milk, Freshwater you can't drink, Needles you can't thread and Newport you can't bottle.

CALLIE: How long does it take to get from London to Cornwall?
FATHER: About six hours.
CALLIE: And from Cornwall to London?
FATHER: The same, of course.
CALLIE: Well, it's not the same from Christmas to Easter as it is from Easter to Christmas, is it?

PASSENGER: Do you stop at the Ritz Hotel?
BUS DRIVER: What! On my salary? You must be joking!

WYNNE: Do you have trouble making up your mind where to go for your holiday?
GWYN: Well, yes and no.

It was a wet day so Dad suggested they made a kite. 'What kind of paper shall we use?' he asked.

'Er, fly paper?' suggested his son.

LARGE LADY: They say travel broadens the mind.
SMALL LADY: If you're anything to go by that's not all it broadens.

Cindy sent a postcard to her friend Lindy. It read: Having a wonderful time. Wish I could afford it!

What do you call a male insect in Scotland?
A laddie bug.

'His nose is so big that while on a walking holiday in Scotland he caught a cold in England.'

'I wouldn't say our landlady was mean, but she keeps a fork in the sugar.'

'Our holiday cottage was so damp that when we set a mousetrap we caught a fish.'

'The hotel advertised bed and board. The trouble was, we didn't know which was which.'

How did the farmer count his cows?
With a cowculator.

The Shufflebottom family had spent an enjoyable holiday on a farm the previous year, and were wondering whether to go there again. 'The only problem,' said Mrs

Shufflebottom, 'was the smell of the pigs.' So
before booking she wrote to the farmer
asking if they still kept pigs.

He replied, 'We haven't had any pigs on
the farm since you stayed here last year.'

What happened when the farmer's cows
escaped from their field?
There was udder chaos.

A city boy visiting the country told his mum,
'That farmer's a magician.'
'What makes you say that?' she replied.
'He just told me he was going
to turn his cows into a field.'

LAURA: Why did you come home early
from your farm holiday?
DORA: Well, the first day we were there a
cow died and we had beef for dinner. The
second day a pig died and we had pork. The
third day the farmer died so we left.

What did the koala take on holiday?
Just the bear essentials.

Why are polar bears white?
They can't sunbathe in the Arctic.

FIRST SCOTSMAN: I went to a travel agent
asking where I could go for £20.
SECOND SCOTSMAN: And?
FIRST SCOTSMAN: And they told me!

Have you read *Enjoying Summer* by Clement
Weather?

A boy holidaying in the countryside went
swimming in a privately owned stretch of
river. He was spotted by a gamekeeper who
yelled, 'Oi! You can't swim here!'
'I'm not swimming,' gasped the boy, 'I'm
trying to stop myself from drowning.'

Little Timmy found a grass snake slithering
through the undergrowth. 'Mum!' he yelled.
'Come quickly! I've found a tail without a body!'

A tourist visiting an English village asked
one of the local inhabitants, 'And have you
lived here all your life?'
The old man grinned. 'Not yet I haven't.'

How many famous people were born in Torquay?
None, only babies were born there.

FIRST GLASWEGIAN: I was going on a trip to London so I thought I'd travel by plane to get there early.
SECOND GLASWEGIAN: And did you?
FIRST GLASWEGIAN: No, I was a day late. The plane went to New York.

The same visitor asked a village lad the time. 'Twelve o'clock,' replied the boy.

'Only twelve o'clock,' said the tourist. 'I thought it was later than that.'

'No,' said the lad, 'it never gets later than that in these parts.'

'Why's that?' asked the tourist.

'Well, after twelve the clock goes back to one.'

A car stopped at a crossroads and the driver leaned out and asked a passerby, 'Which way to Bath?'

'I always use soap and water,' he replied.

Gemma and her parents were setting out on a car trip. 'Can you just check the indicators are working?' asked her dad.

Gemma jumped out and ran round to the back of the car. 'Yes, no, yes, no, yes, no,' she replied.

Ravi and Ronnie were on a camping holiday and were being eaten alive by mosquitoes, so they snuggled down in their sleeping bags to try to avoid them. Ravi poked his head out to see what was happening and saw some fireflies. 'It's no use,' he called back, 'they're coming after us with torches now.'

Tilly and Tolly had rented a cottage by the sea for a week. One day they were sitting in the garden when they saw the council dustcart collecting the bin bags.

'Quick!' said Tilly. 'We forgot the rubbish! Grab that bag and give it to me!'

Tilly rushed up to the dustcart and said, 'Is it too late for the rubbish?'

'No,' said the dustman, 'jump in.'

Mr and Mrs Wittering arrived back late one night at their guesthouse to find all the lights were out. They knocked on the door, at first quietly then, when nothing happened, more loudly. Eventually a window opened and a head stuck out. 'What do you want?' it enquired angrily.

'We're the Witterings and we're staying here,' said Mr Wittering.

'Well, stay there then,' snapped the head, shutting the window and disappearing.

'Our landlord was one in a million.'
'Thank goodness for that!'

Mr and Mrs Dodder were driving through Devon when they decided to stop at an inn for the night. They drew up outside a pub called the George and Dragon and walked in. 'Have you a room for the night?' they asked the landlady.

'No, I'm too busy,' she snapped, and walked away.

So they left and drove around for a while, but couldn't find anywhere else open.

'What shall we do?' asked Mrs Dodder.

'Let's go back,' suggested Mr Dodder, 'and I'll go in and ask to speak to George this time.'

STRANGER IN TOWN: Is that fishmonger in the high street any good?
LOCAL MAN: It seems so. Half a million flies can't be wrong.

ANNOUNCEMENT AT THE BOATING LAKE: Come in, boat number 9.
ATTENDANT: Hang on, we haven't got a boat number 9.
ANNOUNCER: Oh dear, are you in trouble, boat number 6?

FREDDIE: Where have you been?
NEDDIE: You know that fast-food supermarket?
FREDDIE: Yes.
NEDDIE: I spent forty-five minutes looking for the instant coffee.

24

JOCK: What is large, black, with pincers and yellow spots?
JACK: I've no idea. Why do you ask?
JOCK: There's one crawling down your neck.

PAT: Your face reminds me of a Blackpool hotel in January.
NAT: Why?
PAT: Because it's vacant.

What do you get when you cross a mosquito with a knight?
A bite in shining armour.

'Mosquito bites, sunburn, upset tummy – if I didn't need a holiday so much I'd go home.'

GORDON: Where've you been?
JORDAN: I went to see Jonathan off.
GORDON: And was he?
JORDAN: I'll say!

Why is an art gallery like a home for retired teachers?
They're both full of old masters.

NED: What did you think of the Venus de Milo?
TED: **She seemed perfectly 'armless.**

MUSEUM OFFICIAL: You must leave your umbrella in the cloakroom.
VISITOR: **But I haven't got an umbrella.**
MUSEUM OFFICIAL: Then you can't come in. No one can come in without leaving their umbrella in the cloakroom.

JULIE: Did you see that statue called 'The Thinker'?
JULES: **Yes. I wonder what he's thinking about?**
JULIE: He's probably wondering where he left his clothes!

Dad and little Eric were looking at a stuffed bear in a glass case in a museum.

    'Dad,' asked Eric, 'how did they shoot the bear without breaking the glass?'

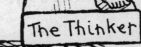

MR KNOWALL: Did you manage to see some of the sights in Paris? The Venus de Milo, for example?

MR WOULDBEKNOWALL: See her? I shook hands with her!

Johnny and Donny were on a camping holiday and had a row over whose turn it was to do the washing-up. Finally, Johnny did it, and retired to bed in a sulk. Donny went for a walk, but very soon he began to feel lonely. So he went back to the camp and pulled back the tent flap.

'Are you awake?' he asked the form curled up in its sleeping-bag.

'I'm not telling you,' came the grumpy reply.

Travelling Around
Sign language

ON A FRENCH HOTEL:
Hot and cold running in all rooms.

ON AN ITALIAN MENU:
Fungus with garlic and persil.

IN AN EGYPTIAN HOTEL:
It is forbidden to steal hotel towels. If you
are not the person to do such please do not
read this notice.

ON A CZECH SHOP WINDOW:
Half-day closing all day Thursday.

IN A BELGIAN HOTEL:
In case of fire please do your utmost to
alarm the hotel porter.

AT A PORTUGUESE BUS STATION:
The comfort of our buses is next to none.

ON A LUGGAGE-HANDLING SERVICE'S ADVERT:

We send your luggage in all directions.

IN A HOTEL RESTAURANT:

If you are satisfactory, please tell your friends. If you are unsatisfactory, please tell the manager.

IN A MOROCCAN HOTEL:

If you have any problems with hotel services, please contact the manager immediately. Do not wait until the last minute, it will then be too late to arrange inconvenience.

IN A HOTEL LIFT:

On the tenth floor is the dining room with magnificent views over the bay. Take the lift and press the tenth bottom now.

IN A GERMAN HOTEL:
Please wash your hans after leaving the toilet.

IN A GERMAN CAFÉ:
Please do not occupy seats in this café
without consuming them.

IN A SWISS HOTEL:
If you require room service, please open
room door and shout, 'Room service!'

IN A MONTE CARLO HOTEL:
Sports jackets may be worn
in the dining room but
no trousers.

IN A SPANISH HOTEL:
In the event of fire, avoid panic, please walk
down corridor to warm the chambermaid.

IN AN ITALIAN MUSEUM:
We must draw attention to our famous
collection of rare beetles, modestly encased
in drawers.

ON AN ESCALATOR:
Lift out of order. Please use elevator.

IN A MEXICAN HOTEL:
Visitors are requested not to throw coffee or other matter into the basin. It stuffs the place inconvenient for the other world.

ON A SPANISH SUPERMARKET:
Open 24 hours except between 1 a.m and 6 a.m.

ON AN ITALIAN PARKING METER:
Parking restricted to 60 minutes in any hour.

ON A ROAD SIGN:
To relieve traffic digestion in the town centre take the ferry every 30 minutes.

ON A SPANISH BEACH:
Persons frequenting this beach are obliged to wear bathing costumes not giving offence to the morals.

IN A GREEK GUIDE BOOK:
Although every care has been taken in the preparation of this guide book we cannot except responsibilities for inoccuracies.

What makes the Tower of Pisa lean?
It doesn't eat much.

DAVE: How did your dad manage to eat the minestrone through his moustache?
MAVE: It was a bit of a strain.

What kind of umbrella does an Italian carry when it's raining?
A wet one.

Where do elephants go on holiday?
Tuskany.

ERIC: How did you like Venice?
DEREK: Oh, I only stayed a few days. The whole place was flooded.

TINA: I'm glad I wasn't born in Italy.
EDWINA: Why?
TINA: I can't speak Italian.

What's Italian, sixty metres high, and full of tomatoes and olives?
The Leaning Tower of Pizza.

Why is Sicily like the letter T?
Because it's in the middle of water.

What does a French chef do when a customer faints?
Gives her the quiche of life.

GALLY: Where did you go for your holidays?
ALLY: France.
GALLY: Which part?
ALLY: All of me.

What's French, wobbly and tastes
delicious?
The Trifle Tower.

What's in the middle of Paris?
The letter R.

An Englishman driving through France
stopped to pick up a hitch-hiker. 'Do
you want a lift?' he enquired.
    'Oui, oui,' replied the
Frenchman.
    'Not in my car you don't,'
said the Englishman, and drove on.

Which French town has two lavatories in
each house?
Toulouse.

'He said he only knew enough French to get
his face slapped.'

'But Mummy, I don't want to go to France.'
'Shut up and keep swimming.'

MAURICE: When we went to Paris we went to the top of the Eiffel Tower.
DORIS: What could you see?
MAURICE: Quite an eyeful!

Why does the River Nile have lots of money?
Because it's got two banks.

'Even if you travel round the world you only move two feet.'

'He booked an all-expenses tour, and that's what it was, all expenses.'

MURPHY: How was your holiday?
MURRAY: I went to the Bahamas and got a wonderful tan. Then I got the bill and turned white.

MRS FLIPPLE: So you're not going to Spain this year?
MRS DIPPLE: No, that was last year. This year we're not going to Turkey.

Where do cats like to go for their holidays?
The Canary Islands.

MR SKINFLINT: My wife wanted to see the world.

MR LOTTADOSH: Did you take her on a trip?

MR SKINFLINT: No, I bought her an atlas.

MRS WALLY: When my husband first saw the Grand Canyon his face dropped a mile.

MRS DOLLY: Was he disappointed?

MRS WALLY: No, he fell over the edge.

Tim and Jim went to stay on a dude ranch in Wyoming for their holidays. They had a wonderful time riding the range, learning how to rope steers, and camping under the stars at night. 'There's just one thing, though,' said Tim to Jim, 'why does the trail boss call me Paleface? I've got quite a suntan.'

'Well, actually,' replied Jim to Tim, 'he told me it was because you had a face like a bucket.'

CHARLIE: What kind of time did you have in New York?

CHESTER: Eastern standard time.

A Scotsman visited Canada. 'What's that animal over there?' he asked.

'That's a moose,' explained his Canadian guide.

'Whew!' exclaimed the Scotsman. 'If that's a moose your rats must be as big as elephants!'

Which country has the thinnest people?
Finland.

What's the coldest country in the world?
Chile.

'I'm going to Florida for the winter. I can't afford an overcoat.'

FRANK: I hear it never rains in Florida.
HANK: No, but the sun drips perspiration.

Mr Smith, who went on a trip to Africa, wrote a postcard to his wife back in England. It read, 'Arrived safely this morning. The heat is terrible.' Unfortunately, it was delivered to another Mrs Smith, the widow of a man who had just died.

What do you get when Batman falls off the Empire State Building?
Splatman.

A tourist went into a shop that developed films and asked if they did life-size enlargements.

'Certainly,' replied the shop-keeper.

'Oh, good,' said the tourist. 'Here's a picture of the Empire State Building.'

A man who wanted to fly from New York to Los Angeles phoned a travel agent to see how long the flight would be.

'Just a minute,' she replied, checking her computer screen.

'Thank you,' answered the man, and hung up.

A woman went into a post office in Chicago and said she wanted to send a parcel to Washington.

'You can't do that, madam,' said the clerk, 'he's been dead for years.'

Where do silly ants live?
Antwerp.

'If the world is round, how can you travel to the four corners of it?'

CHRIS: Mum went to the West Indies last year.
TRIS: Jamaica?
CHRIS: No, she went of her own accord.

What's the silliest amusement park in the world?
Dizzyland.

Where did the idiots go on their skiing trip?
The Sahara Desert.

A traveller was looking round a Cairo market. 'What is that?' he asked, pointing at what looked like a human skull.

'That is the skull of the great pharoah Cheops,' replied the stallholder.

'And what's this smaller skull?' enquired the traveller.

'That is the skull of the great pharoah Cheops when he was a little boy,' answered the trader.

What kind of joke would you find at the top of the Great Pyramid?
A cone-under-'em (a conundrum).

KELLY: I hear you've been to Switzerland.
SHELLEY: That's right.
KELLY: What did you think of the scenery?
SHELLEY: I couldn't see much of it, there were too many mountains in the way.

What can go all round the world and stay in one corner?
A postage stamp.

Why did the nerd take a water pistol when he went canoeing?
He was going to shoot the rapids.

Ken was on a safari holiday in Africa, and the guide was explaining to his party how to cope with wild animals. 'For example,' he said, 'a lion won't hurt you if you carry a white umbrella.'

'Is that so?' asked Ken. 'But how fast do you have to carry it?'

What's purple and 2,400 kilometres long?
The Grape Wall of China.

OLLY: I wish I hadn't swapped my car for a holiday in Bermuda.
DOLLY: Because now you realize you need a car to travel around in?
OLLY: No, because I want to go on holiday to Australia.

Gilly was not enjoying her holiday in Spain. Her friend Billy asked her, 'Are you homesick?'
'No,' said Gilly, 'I'm here-sick.'

DARREN: Mum, why can't I go swimming?
MUM: There are sharks in the water.
DARREN: But Dad's swimming!
MUM: He's insured.

Mr and Mrs Sparrowshanks went on holiday
to Russia, where they were shown round
Moscow by a guide called Rudolph.

When they were in the Kremlin, Mr
Sparrowshanks looked out of the window
and said, 'Oh, look, it's snowing.'

'That's not snow, it's rain,' said the guide
Rudolph.

'I'm sure it's snow,' persisted Mr
Sparrowshanks.

'No, it's definitely rain,' replied the guide.

Mr Sparrowshanks began to speak again
when his wife put a hand on his arm. 'I'm
sure,' she said, 'that Rudolph the Red knows
rain, dear.'

On the Beach

ANDY: I love the sun.
MANDY: Oh, so do I. I could sit in the sun all day and all night.

MUM: You're squinting in the sun. Why not move out of it?
MEG: Why should I? I was here first.

Who on the beach has the biggest sunhat?
The person with the biggest head.

TILLY: I got terribly sunburned on holiday.
MILLY: Well, I guess you basked for it.

When it comes to sunbathing ignorance is blister.

Jim and Tim were paddling in the sea. Jim said, 'Coo! Aren't your feet dirty!'
    'Well,' said Tim, 'we didn't come here last year.'

Little Susie looked at her peeling suntan and said, 'I'm only seven and I'm wearing out already.'

One Easter holiday a man walking along the beach with his dog met a little boy. The boy wore a pair of long football socks, and was paddling in the sea.

'I couldn't help wondering,' said the man, 'why are you paddling wearing socks?'

'Oh,' replied the boy, 'the water's not very warm at this time of year.'

Tommy said to a lifeguard, 'Can I swim in the sea?'

'Yes,' replied the lifeguard.

'That's odd,' said Tommy, 'I can't swim in the swimming pool at school.'

DAVE: What did you do on holiday?
MAVE: We went to see the sea.
DAVE: Did the sea see you?
MAVE: Well, it waved at us.

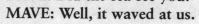

A man climbed a cliff and got stuck, so he shouted for help. When another man came to rescue him he said, 'Can't you get down the same way you got up there?'

'No,' said the climber, 'I came up head first.'

'It was so hot when we were on holiday we took turns to sit in each other's shadow.'

'Our holiday resort was so dull that one day the tide went out and never came back again.'

FREDA: You've got a wonderful tan.
FIONA: I should have, I reckon it cost £25 per square centimetre.

BILLY: Where did you learn to swim?
GILLY: In the water.

RON: Our holiday house was a stone's throw from the beach.
DON: That was handy.
RON: Yes. And very easy to find – all its windows were broken.

A man went swimming and all his clothes were stolen. What did he come home in?
The dark.

SALLY: Why did you wear your bathing suit in the Sahara? There's no water there.
WALLY: No, but what a beach!

What leaves yellow footprints on the seabed?
A lemon sole.

What goes in pink and comes out blue?
Someone bathing in the sea at Christmas.

NEDDIE: What's the difference between a holiday in Spain, a piggy bank and a tube of glue?
TEDDY: I don't know. What is the difference?
NEDDIE: A holiday in Spain is sunny, a piggy bank holds money . . . .
TEDDY: But what about the tube of glue?
NEDDIE: Ah, I thought that's where you'd get stuck.

Knock, knock.
Who's there?
Felix.
Felix who?
Felixcited about going on holiday.

BERT: Why are you limping?
GERT: A crab pinched my toe.
BERT: Which one?
GERT: I don't know. All crabs look the same to me.

Did you hear about the deep-sea diver coming up who passed his boat going down?

What lurks at the bottom of the sea and makes you an offer you can't refuse?
The Codfather.

Who has a six-shooter and terrorizes the ocean?
Billy the Squid.

Who was the world's first underwater spy?
James Pond.

What swims through the sea at 100 mph?
A motorpike.

What animal hunts mice in the sea?
A catfish.

Why does the ocean roar?
It has crabs in its bed.

JEN: Is your watch waterproof?
KEN: Yes. Any water that gets in it never gets out again.

What's the definition of a
bathing beauty?
A girl worth wading for.

LONNIE: Did you see that
girl over there?
DONNIE: Yes, her bathing
suit fitted like a suntan.

JAYNE: You remind me
of the sea.
WAYNE: Because I'm exciting and romantic?
JAYNE: No, because you make me sick.

What do you call a wicked woman who lives
near the sea?
A sand witch.

Did you hear about the man who talked so
much that when he went to the beach he had
to put suntan lotion on his tongue?

WINSTON: Why are you doing the backstroke?
WINIFRED: I've just had lunch and you're not supposed to swim on a full stomach.

Knock, knock.
Who's there?
Ma.
Ma who?
Ma swimsuit's split and I daren't get out of the water.

'What's so wonderful about seeing the sea? When you've seen one sea you've seen all of them.'

How do you cut through waves?
With a sea-saw.

BOYD: Did you enjoy your holiday with your cousin?
LLOYD: Yes. We took turns to bury each other in the sand.
BOYD: Sounds fun.
LLOYD: It was. And next year I'm going back to dig her up.

ANDY: My sister said she had nothing to wear for her holidays.
ARTHUR: And was that true?
ANDY: I'm not sure, but she's got three wardrobes to keep it in.

What dashes round the seabed chasing crooks?
A squid car.

What sea creature is good at maths?
An octoplus.

Why did the crab blush?
Because the seaweed.

What did one rockpool say to the other?
'Show us your mussels.'

Jack and Jill were on holiday with their parents and Auntie Vera, whom they found a bit of a drag. So when, after a week, she announced, 'I think I'll go home tomorrow. Will you be sorry?' Jill was surprised to hear Jack answer 'yes'.

Afterwards Jill said to him, 'I thought you always told the truth. You lied to Auntie Vera.'

'No I didn't,' answered Jack. 'I'd been hoping she was going home today.'

Knock, knock.
Who's there?
Godfrey.
Godfrey who?
Godfrey tickets for a trip to the seaside.

How do teddies send their holiday postcards?
By bear mail.

Did you hear about the loony who sat on the beach all night trying to work out what happened to the sun when it went down? It finally dawned on him.

Out and About

BERNIE: Have you ever been lost?
ERNIE: My parents nearly lost me once on holiday.
BERNIE: What happened?
ERNIE: They didn't take me far enough into the woods.

CHAZZA: I hear Kate's gone to her pen friend's in Switzerland for a month.
BAZZA: Does she need a holiday?
CHAZZA: No, but her parents do.

'How was your week's skiing?'
'Interesting. I spent one day skiing and six in hospital.'

A local was describing the beauty of the scenery to a tourist. 'You see those mountains?' he asked. 'Well, they're the highest in the world except for those in foreign parts.'

A very rich lady hired a limousine and chauffeur to drive her round the sights on her holiday. 'What's your name?' she asked the chauffeur.

'Fred, madam,' answered the driver.

'I always call my chauffeurs by their surnames,' said the lady. 'What's yours?'

'Darling, madam,' he answered.

'Drive on, Fred.'

WENDY: Look at all the water in that lake.
WINNIE: Yes, and that's only the top of it.

A boy saw a man fishing by the riverbank. 'Is this river any good for fish?' he asked.

'It must be,' replied the fisherman, 'because I can't get any of them to leave it.'

FIRST FISHERMAN: Have you caught anything?
SECOND FISHERMAN: Yes. I caught a fish a metre long but then I remembered that our frying pan is only twenty centimetres wide so I threw it back.

CLARA: I went on a fishing holiday.
SARAH: Did you catch anything?
CLARA: Yes, sunburn and mosquito bites.

ANITA: How many fish have you caught today?
PETER: When I get another I'll have caught one.

Mr and Mrs Woofle were on a safari holiday in Kenya when a lion sprang on Mrs Woofle.
    'Shoot, Wilfred, shoot!' she screamed.
    'I can't,' he replied. 'I've run out of film.'

DICK: I hear you climbed Mont Blanc on your holidays.
NICK: That's right.
DICK: Did you get to the top?
NICK: No. We were about fifty metres from the top when we ran out of scaffolding.

EMMA: Did you enjoy your pony trekking?
GEMMA: Yes, except when the pony wanted to go one way and I wanted to go another.
EMMA: What happened?
GEMMA: We tossed for it.

'I'm going on holiday to the mountains for my health. That's where I left it last year.'

SURESH: How did you get on with your surf riding?
STEVIE: Not very well. I couldn't get the horse to go in the water.

MRS BLACK: I sent my husband to the seaside for his holiday.
MRS WHITE: And did he enjoy it?
MRS BLACK: I don't know, but I certainly did!

JULIE: Is it raining outside?
JULIAN: Does it ever rain inside?

What do you call a crazy golfer?
A crack putt.

Knock, knock.
Who's there?
Ammonia.
Ammonia who?
Ammonia going to Scotland, so I don't need a passport.

Why didn't the dumbo enjoy his water skiing holiday?
He couldn't find a sloping lake.

A man went to a riding stables and said, 'I'd like to hire a horse.'

'Certainly,' answered the proprietor. 'How long?'

'The longest you've got,' replied the man. 'I've got four children.'

How *do* you hire a horse?
Stand it on four bricks.

SHEILA: You've put your
ski boots on the wrong feet.
SHIRLEY: They're the only feet I've got.

NEVILLE: Can we take a ladder with us on holiday?
MUM: Whatever for?
NEVILLE: Dad says we're going to do some climbing.

The Muggins family went on a walking holiday and young Mark complained bitterly about his aching feet and his blisters.

'You're hopeless!' said his father. 'When I was your age I thought nothing of walking fifteen miles a day!'

'I don't think much of it either,' replied Mark.

A man climbing a mountain fell down 100 metres, breaking several bones in the process. When the mountain rescue people came they said to him, 'Hang on to this rope and we'll pull you up.'

But the man explained he couldn't do that because he'd broken both arms.

'OK,' said the rescuer, 'get hold of it with your teeth.'

So the man put the rope in his teeth, and slowly and painfully his rescuer began to drag him to safety. 'Are you all right?' he called down.

'Yes,' replied the climber, 'aaaaaahhhhhh.'

Knock, knock.
Who's there?
Shirley.
Shirley who?
Shirley we must be
near the top of the
mountain by now!

RYAN: We're going
on a ferry on our
holiday.
BRYAN: Every time I go on a ferry it makes
me cross.

Mike went on a flying course for his holidays. 'Have you any experience of flying?' asked his instructor.

'Well, I did once fall out of a window,' he replied.

TRAVEL AGENT: And where do you want to go, sir?

TOURIST: I want to travel where the hand of man has never set foot.

JEFF: If you go to the zoo don't forget to buy two tickets.
JOHN: Why?
JEFF: One to get in and one to get out again.

JAYNE: When I went to that dance I met the ugliest girl I'd ever seen.
WAYNE: You forget yourself, dear.

SALLY: Did you enjoy your holiday with the Jollys?
WALLY: No. Their idea of a good evening's entertainment was putting out the rubbish.

BOY AT DISCO: May I have the last dance?
GIRL AT DISCO: You've just had it!

What book tells you where you can go on holiday?
Your chequebook!

A man went into the bar at an old-fashioned golf club. 'Do you serve wives in this bar?' he asked.

'No, sir,' replied the barman. 'You'll have to bring your own.'

Little Lenny managed to swallow his dad's roll of film. His dad rushed him to the local hospital, where the doctor examined him and said, 'Don't worry. We'll keep him in for a day or two and see what develops.'

Knock, knock.
Who's there?
Sal.
Sal who?
Sal long way to New Zealand!

TERRY: You've spent all day shopping! What have you got?
KERRY: Sore feet and a headache.

MANDY: Was it crowded at the disco last night?
SANDY: Not under my table.

Have you read *Travelling from London to Timbuctoo* by Miles Apart?

Knock, knock.
Who's there?
Europe.
Europe who?
Europe early this morning!

Young Andy had spent a week at scout camp and when he returned his dad asked if he'd learned to tie any knots.

'Oh yes,' he replied enthusiastically. 'And next week we're going back to untie the scout master!'

Table Talk

FRED: How was the restaurant?
TED: It was not so much a restaurant as a bureau of missing portions.

BRITISH TOURIST IN AMERICA: What's the difference between the $5 steak and the $10 steak?
WAITER: $5.

TOURIST IN ITALY: I'd like some of what is written on the menu, please.
WAITER: The band is playing it now, sir.

'The restaurant was so expensive I took one look at the menu and lost my appetite.'

'Our waiter was so rude! When I ordered alphabet soup he read it over my shoulder.'

WAITER: How did you find your lunch, sir?
DINER: With a magnifying glass.

KERRY: Is there modern air-conditioning in the restaurant?
JERRY: You could call it that. The waiter waves a menu in your face.

'I ordered hot chocolate and the waiter brought me a Mars bar and a box of matches.'

DINER: There's an alarm clock in my food!
WAITER: Well, you did ask for chicken tikka.

DINER: How long have you worked here?
WAITER: Just six months, sir.
DINER: Then it can't be you who took my order.

DINER: This food is terrible!
Bring me the manager!
WAITER: He's not on the menu.

'What's this?'
'It's bean soup.'
'I don't care what it's been, what is it now?'

SIGN IN A CAFE: Today's special: **pot of tea with stones, jam and cream £2.**

How can you make a chicken stew?
Keep it waiting for hours.

The Brown family were on holiday in Switzerland. Little Billy Brown wrinkled his nose when the cheese was brought.

'I don't like cheese with holes in,' he said.

'Never mind,' said his mother soothingly. 'Leave them at the side of your plate.'

'Do I have to sit here until I die of starvation?'
'No, we throw you out at closing time.'

Donnie was staying in a bed-and-breakfast guest house and when he came down in the morning a delicious smell of cooking filled the air. 'Mmm,' he said appreciatively, 'is that bacon I smell?'

'It is,' replied his landlady, 'and you do.'

A man walked into a chip shop. 'Fish and chips twice,' he ordered.

'I heard you the first time,' said the proprietor.

'Waiter, have you any wild strawberries?'
'No, but I could irritate some tame ones for you.'

'Should you eat sushi with your fingers?'
'No, fingers should be eaten separately.'

What did the man say when he walked into the bar?
'Ouch!'

Two men walked into a bar and the first one said, 'A beer for Donkey and me.'

The landlord served the beer and said to the second man, 'Why does he call you Donkey?'

The second man replied, 'Eeyore, eeyore, eeyore'll ways calls me that.'

Another man went into a pub and ordered a whisky. He drank it and left without paying.

The following week he went back to the pub. 'Just a minute,' said the landlord, 'you're the man who came in here last week, had a whisky and left without paying for it.'

'No,' said the man, 'that wasn't me.'

'Well,' replied the landlord, 'you must have a double.'

'Thanks very much,' said the man. 'I'll have a scotch.'

Three hikers stopped outside a café, and one went in to get a thermos flask filled.

'What would you like in it?' asked the assistant.

'I'd like three coffees, please,' said the hiker. 'Two with milk and sugar and one without.'

'It looks like rain this morning,' said the guest-house landlord, as he served the breakfast coffee.

'It tastes like it too,' replied a guest, sipping the coffee.

MRS MACKIE: I feel like a cup of tea.
MRS MICKIE: You look like one too – all wet and weak.

DINER: Did you serve me some spaghetti?
WAITER: No, sir.
DINER: Oh dear, I must have eaten your wormery.

DINER: Those peas were very hard.
WAITER: You've just eaten your wife's necklace, sir.

SAMMY: You owe me £2 for that honey.
TAMMY: What, honey? I didn't know you cared!

TOURIST IN FRANCE: Do you have frogs' legs?
WAITER: No, sir, it's just the way I walk.

BASIL: This restaurant must have a very clean kitchen.
BERTIE: Why do you say that?
BASIL: Everything tastes of soap.

LIZZIE: We had a goose for dinner on our farm holiday and everyone was tickled.
LINDY: Why was that?
LIZZIE: The farmer had forgotten to pluck it.

HARRY: Do you eat slugs?
LARRY: Of course not. Why do you ask?
HARRY: There's one in your sandwich.

Susie and Sally went for lunch with their Auntie Brenda when they were on their holiday. Their mother gave them a glass of sherry to take to her, and when they had done so, they stood and stared at her.

'What's the matter?' asked Auntie Brenda.

'We're waiting to see you do your trick,' explained Susie.

'What's that?' asked Auntie Brenda.

'Mum says you drink like a fish,' explained Sally.

Why is it hard to buy honey in Bournemouth?
There's only one bee in Bournemouth.

'We ate health food on our holiday.'
'Did it make you healthy?'
'No, you had to be healthy
to survive it.'

How long does an Italian cook
spaghetti?
Oh, about thirty centimetres.

How does an Italian eat spaghetti?
He puts it in his mouth and chews.

Why can't you starve in the desert?
Because of the sand which is there.

66

DINER: I'd like a hamburger, please.
WAITER: With pleasure.
DINER: No, just with the usual relish, please.

VICKY: Our Dad believes in a balanced diet.
MICKY: Is that why he always has a glass of beer in each hand?

BRENDA: That restaurant's got an interesting item on the menu.
GLENDA: What's that?
BRENDA: Soup in a basket!

The Bumbles were having tea in a café and the waitress offered a sandwich to little Bertha Bumble. 'Thank you very much,' said Bertha.

'I do like to hear polite children say "thank you",' said the waitress.

Mrs Bumble smiled, but Bertha said, 'If you want to hear me say it again, you could offer me a piece of cake.'

DINER: I'd like the roast beef, please, and make it lean.
WAITER: Certainly, sir, which way?

What do you call fake spaghetti?
Mockoroni.

Seeing the World

A man went to equatorial Africa. 'I've come here for the winter,' he explained.

'There isn't any winter here,' said one of the local inhabitants.

Where do wasps come from?
Stingapore.

What do you call a mosquito on holiday?
An itch-hiker.

'You know,' said Mr Jones to Mrs Jones, 'we've been in Paris for six days and we haven't visited the Louvre yet.'

'I know, dear,' replied Mrs Jones to Mr Jones. 'I expect it's the change of water.'

A woman went into a Paris post office to buy a stamp for her postcard. 'Do I have to stick this on myself?' she asked the clerk. 'No, on the postcard,' he replied.

SIGN IN A PARIS HOTEL:
If you wish to change in Paris
please do so at the hotel bank.

What happened to the man who
jumped off a bridge in Paris?
He went in Seine.

'When I was on holiday I met a
Spanish lady who had twins. She
couldn't tell Juan from the other.'

What sport can you watch in
Transylvania?
Drac racing.

HUGH: What's the name of that place you
went to in China, where they make car
hooters?
LEW: Hong King.

Who wrote *Cruising in the Arctic Ocean*?
I. C. Waters.

Which country suffers from aches?
Spain.

Why did the egg go into the jungle?
Because it was an eggsplorer.

Where do ghosts go on holiday?
The Dead Sea.

What's an exact duplicate of Texas?
The Clone Star State.

Which country sells more
stone than any other?
Morocco (more-rock-o).

'Do you suffer from seasickness?'
'**I'll say. When I went to Venice I got queasy
crossing the street.**'

What did the tourist say when he went for a
haircut in Germany?
'**Good morning, Herr Dresser.**'

What did the French musician say when he
saw the white cliffs of Dover?
'**Cor, anglais.**'

How does an Eskimo build a house?
'**E glues it together.**

MR SOLLY: What a storm there was last
night! I never saw such rain!
MRS SOLLY: Why didn't you wake me? You
know I can never sleep through a storm!

GEORGE: My Dad faced a tiger in India and didn't turn a hair.
GLORIA: I'm not surprised. He's completely bald!

COLONEL BLIMP: If you go to the jungle, don't play cards.
COLONEL BLUMP: Why not?
COLONEL BLIMP: There are too many cheetahs.

MIKE: I wonder what that tiger would say if he could talk?
SPIKE: He'd probably say he was a leopard.

What's a Laplander?
A clumsy man on a busy bus.

JIM: What's the weather forecast?
JOHN: Part sunny, part cloudy, part accurate.

How can you tell the time by the sun?
Shade your eyes and look at your watch.

Little Eric was taken to church when he was on holiday and when he returned his mother asked if he'd behaved himself.

'Oh, yes,' he replied. 'I was very good. Someone offered me a plate of money and I said "no thanks".'

Mrs Twillytoe took little Tilda to an art gallery, and was surprised to find her hitting a statue with her belt.

'What on earth are you doing?' asked Mrs Twillytoe.

'Well,' replied Tilda, 'I was looking at this statue when the attendant came round and told me to beat it.'

The Thinker

'How did you find the weather when you were on holiday?'
'Oh, I just went outside and there it was.'

HEATHER: What was the weather like in the Alps?
HOLLY: Different. It was the only place I've been where you get a suntan over your frostbite.

NINA: Shut the door, it's cold outside.
TINA: Will that make it warmer outside?

ELTON: Why do you wear sunglasses on rainy days?
ELLA: To keep umbrellas out of my eyes.

HARRY: I blew into town yesterday.
LARRY: Strong wind?

GAME WARDEN: I shall have to arrest you for swimming in that lake.
SWIMMER: You might have told me before I changed into my swimsuit!
GAME WARDEN: There's no law against that!

Who wrote *The Worst Journey in the World*?
Helen Back.

Where did the bad choir go on holiday?
Singapore.

Mr and Mrs Whittlebury were taking young Walter on a car drive, and young Walter didn't enjoy long drives. So Mrs Whittlebury said to him, 'If you're good I'll give you a shiny new 50p piece.'

Walter thought for a moment. 'Could you make it a dirty old £1 coin?'

A man who had had too much to drink asked a tourist, 'Is that the sun or the moon?'
The tourist replied, 'I don't know, I don't live round here.'

KAREN: Why do you always take your holidays in the spring?
SHARON: The sheets are cleaner.

MR DUM: Did you to go Spain for your holidays?
MR DIM: I don't know, my wife bought the tickets.

MUM: Haven't you got any friends here to play with?
LEO: Yes, but I hate them.

MUM: Why are you writing that postcard so slowly?
DAVE: It's for Granny. She's a slow reader.

Johnny and Julie were staying with their granny in the country. 'Would you like to see the cuckoo come out of the cuckoo clock?' she asked them.

'We'd rather see Grandfather come out of the grandfather clock,' they replied.

'Was it difficult to take her photo?'
'No, it was a snap.'

MARY: I don't like this photo. It doesn't do me justice.
CARY: **It's mercy you want, not justice.**

BOBBIE: Did you go to Cornwall for your holidays, stupid?
ROBBIE: **Yes, and I came back stupid too.**

TOMMY: Where did you go on holiday?
TIMMY: **I'm not sure until I've had my films developed.**

AL: After the holiday I'm going to start work as a baker.
VAL: **Why?**
AL: I knead the dough.

If a man is born in Italy, educated in Greece, lived in America and died in Britain, what is he?
Dead.

Did you hear about the man who always wore sunglasses?
He took a dim view of everything.

Young Tommy was staying on a farm with his parents and discovered the apple orchard. He'd climbed up a tree and had an apple in his hand when the farmer spotted him.

'What are you doing up that tree, young man?' he asked suspiciously.

'Er,' stammered Tommy, 'one of your apples fell down and I'm putting it back.'

A man on the top diving board of the hotel swimming pool was poised to jump when the pool attendant rushed up and yelled, 'Don't jump! There's no water in the pool!'

'That's all right,' answered the man cheerfully. 'I can't swim.'

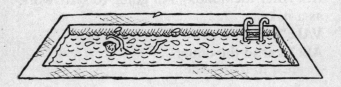

MRS TWINKLE: If it's raining, let's hurry on our walk.
MR TWINKLE: Will that make it rain less?

Where do holidaymakers go when they have a cough?
The theatre.

A gamekeeper spotted a man swimming in a river. 'Come out of the water,' he shouted, 'there's no bathing allowed here.'

'I'm not bathing,' gurgled the man, 'I'm drowning.'

GAMEKEEPER: No fishing is allowed here.
LITTLE BOY: I'm not fishing, I'm giving my pet worm a bath.

JOHNNY: What did you do in Austria?
RONNIE: I thought of going skiing but I decided to let it slide.

TOURIST IN USA: Can you lend me $5? I want to phone a friend back home in England.
AMERICAN: Here's $10. Phone all your friends in England.

A tourist driving through Surrey slowed down when he saw a passer-by and called out of the window, 'Leatherhead?'

'Monkey face!' came the reply.

TIM: Did you meet a nice girl at the dance?
JIM: Yes. She has lots of personality.
TIM: Mine wasn't very good-looking either!

A woman in Rome went into a bank to cash a traveller's cheque. 'Can you identify yourself?' asked the cashier.

The woman rummaged in her handbag, took out a small mirror, looked at her reflection, and said, 'Yes, that's me.'

A tourist in the Middle East asked a guide, 'Where was Solomon's Temple?'

'On the side of his head,' replied the guide.

A hiker asked a man walking a dog, 'Will this path take me to the seafront?'

'No,' answered the man. 'You'll have to go by yourself.'

Ginny went on a rock-climbing holiday. Faced with a particularly sheer cliff, she asked her instructor nervously, 'Do people often fall off here?'

'No,' he replied, 'once is usually enough.'

A Place to Stay

Knock, knock.
Who's there?
Noah.
Noah who?
Noah good place to stay in this town?

JENNY: They said our hotel was just five
minutes from Sorrento.
KENNY: And wasn't it?
JENNY: Possibly – by phone.

HOTEL GUEST: Hmm, the room's not bad
but I'd like one with a bath.
**HOTEL MANAGER: This isn't your room,
sir, it's the lift.**

The hotel manager was telling a new porter
how to make guests feel at home. 'Be
friendly towards them, call them by their
names,' he said.

'Right, sir. And if I don't know their

names?' asked the porter.

'Just check the labels on their luggage,' explained the manager.

Later, the porter decided to try out this tactic. He picked up a couple of smart suitcases, glanced at the labels, and headed towards the lift. 'Pleased to meet you, Mr and Mrs Louis Vuitton,' he smiled.

HOTEL GUEST: Are the rooms here quiet?
HOTEL MANAGER: Of course, sir. It's only the guests who are noisy.

JOHN: How was your hotel?
DON: Oh, great. They had three swimming pools.
JOHN: Three?
DON: Yes. One had hot water, one had cold water, the third had no water at all.
JOHN: What use was that?
DON: It was for people who can't swim.

HOTEL GUEST: Do these stairs take you to the top floor?
HOTEL MANAGER: No, I'm afraid you'll have to walk.

HOTEL GUEST: What are your weekly rates?
HOTEL RECEPTIONIST: I don't know. No one's ever stayed that long.

'Our hotel was so run-down they stole towels from the guests.'

HOTEL GUEST: Get out! This isn't your room!
INTRUDER: Sorry, I'm afraid I'm not myself tonight.

HOTEL GUEST: Is that room service? Can you send up a bath towel, please?
HOTEL MAID: Certainly, sir. But can you wait a few minutes, someone else is using it at present.

HOTEL RECEPTIONIST: Do you want a room with a private bath?
HOTEL GUEST: Yes, please, a private bath is the only kind I like.

FIRST GUEST: They say they serve fresh food in this hotel.
SECOND GUEST: And they do! When I asked for a glass of milk they brought a cow into the dining room.

A man rushed into a hotel lobby and asked for a glass of water. When one was brought he rushed off with it, returned a few moments later with it empty, and asked for another one. When he returned with the empty glass a second time, the receptionist asked, 'Why don't you drink the water here?'

'It's not to drink,' gasped the man, 'my room's on fire.'

Two men were discussing their partly built hotels in a Spanish resort. 'And aren't the walls thin!' exclaimed the first.

'I'll say,' agreed the second. 'I asked my wife a question and got four different answers!'

'The lighting in our room had three degrees of brightness – dim, flicker and off.'

'Our hotel had automatic air-conditioning – every time the weather got really hot it automatically broke down.'

'The pianist only knew two tunes. One was "The Bluebells of Scotland" and the other wasn't.'

'If you ask them for a six o'clock call they wake you at five to tell you you have another hour to sleep.'

'They changed the sheets twice a day – from one room to another.'

'They said there was running water in each room but I didn't expect it to come from the ceiling.'

What did one hotel lift say to the other?
'I think I'm going down with something.'

What's brown and carries a suitcase?
A handle.

MRS NUTTER: That's
a strange pair of socks,
one blue and one green.
MR NUTTER: Yes,
isn't it. And I've got
another pair just the
same in my suitcase.

HOTEL GUEST: I'd like a room with a sea
view please.
RECEPTIONIST: They cost £10 extra.
HOTEL GUEST: How much if I promise not
to look?

MRS PETTIGREW: Was yours a big hotel?
MRS PETTITOES: Oh, yes. By the time
you'd walked from reception to your room
you owed them for the first day.

MR TATERS: Was your hotel busy?
MR SPUDS: It was so full I had to sleep
stretched out on a door propped between
two trestles.
MR TATERS: Were you comfortable?
MR SPUDS: Ye-es, but it was a bit draughty
round the letterbox.

MRS TUBBY: Is the hotel air-conditioned?
MR TUBBY: Probably – I've never known
air in this condition.

HOTEL RECEPTION: This is the third time
you've rung. What's eating you?
HOTEL GUEST: That's what I'd like to
know!

JULIE: Did you have a shower in your
room?
JOHNNY: Yes. I stood under it every day for
five minutes.
JULIE: Really?
JOHNNY: Yes. And once a week I turned
it on.

BEN: Last night I dreamed I was eating my
pillow.
LEN: Are you all right now?
BEN: Yes, but I'm a little down in the mouth.

NINA: I've got a nice room and a bath.
TINA: That's all right, then.
NINA: Trouble is, they're in different buildings.

A hotel guest was talking to an elderly man who'd lived in the place for years, but was thinking of moving on.

'What makes you want to move?' asked the guest.

'I found out they didn't have a bath,' replied the elderly resident.

Mr and Mrs Noddle were eating strawberries for tea in their holiday guest house when their landlady's dog came up and wagged his tail at them.

'What a nice, friendly dog,' said Mrs Noddle, patting him on the head. 'He seems to like us.'

'That's probably because you're eating out of his bowl,' replied the landlady.

MR NIDDLE: Why do you always sing in the bathroom?
MRS NIDDLE: Haven't you noticed? There's no lock on the door.

Did you hear about Gwyn and Lynne? They met in the hotel's revolving door and they've been going round together ever since.

A man trekked across the mountains and eventually came to a small, run-down hotel in a tiny village. 'Can I stay the night?' he asked the proprietor.

'Yes, but you'll have to make your own bed,' he replied.

'That's all right,' answered the man.

'Right,' said the proprietor, 'here's a hammer and some nails. You'll find the wood in the toolshed outside.'

HOTEL GUEST: I'd like a room for the night, please.
RECEPTIONIST: Single, sir?
HOTEL GUEST: Yes, but I am engaged to be married.

The hotel prided itself on its restaurant. 'We have almost everything on the menu, sir,' beamed the restaurant manager to a guest.

'So I see,' replied the guest, wrinkling his nose. 'Could you bring me a clean one, please?'

TAMMY: We had a cabaret act at our hotel. A man did animal impressions.
SAMMY: Really? You mean he made the noises?
TAMMY: No, he did the smells!

What's the difference between a dog with fleas and a bored hotel guest?
One's going to itch and the other's itching to go.

DAD: And who managed to break the hotel window?
BEN: It was Harry.
DAD: And how did he do it?
BEN: He ducked when I threw a cricket ball at him.

A man who lived in very remote mountains, where there was no electricity or gas, went on holiday for the first time in his life and stayed in a hotel. When he returned, his friends asked him how he had enjoyed it.

'Oh, it was lovely,' he answered. 'The problem was; I couldn't sleep.'

'Why was that?' asked his friend.

'The light was on in my bedroom all the time.'

'Why didn't you blow it out?'

'I tried to, but it was inside a little glass bottle.'

A man went into a hotel lobby and called out, 'Has anyone lost a roll of £10 notes with a rubber band round it?'

Several people rushed forward.

'Here you are,' said the man to the first claimant. 'I've found your rubber band!'

HOTEL MANAGER: I hope you enjoyed your stay, sir.
HOTEL GUEST, PAYING BILL: Yes, but I'm sorry to leave the hotel so soon after almost buying it.